LIGHTNING BOLT BOOKS™

Do You Know about Birds?

Buffy Silverman

Lerner Publications Company

Minneapolis

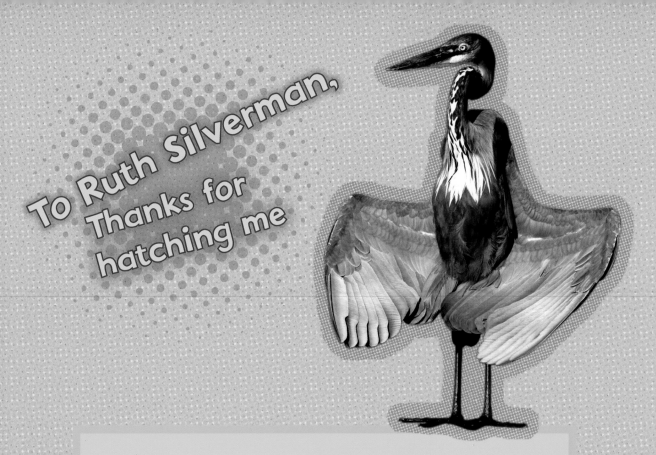

To Ruth Silverman,
Thanks for
hatching me

Lerner Publications Company
A division of Lerner Publishing Group, Inc.
241 First Avenue North
Minneapolis, MN 55401 U.S.A.

Website address: www.lernerbooks.com

Library of Congress Cataloging-in-Publication Data

Silverman, Buffy.
        Do you know about birds — by Buffy Silverman.
            p.   cm. — (Lightning bolt books™ — Meet the animal groups)
        Includes index.
        ISBN 978-0-8225-7541-2 (lib. bdg. : alk. paper)
        1. Birds — Juvenile literature. I. Title.
    QL676.2.S55 2010
        598 — dc22   2007042175

Manufactured in the United States of America
1 2 3 4 5 6 — BP — 15 14 13 12 11 10

Contents

Birds Have Feathers

Have you seen birds in the city? Pigeons on the sidewalk bob their heads. Have you seen birds in the water? Swans paddle across the lake.

Like all birds, pigeons and swans have feathers. Birds are the only animals that have feathers.

This pigeon lives in the city.

A swan swims in the lake.

Feathers help birds stay warm or cool. Birds fluff their down feathers to keep warm. On hot days, they flatten their feathers to cool down.

A blue jay fluffs its feathers to stay warm.

Smooth body feathers cover down feathers. Body feathers overlap, so water runs off them.

Body feathers help keep this duck dry.

Some birds have feathers that help them hide.

Can you spot this woodcock?

Other birds have brightly colored feathers.

A peacock shows off his feathers.

9

What do birds use to fly?

Flight feathers!

Birds spread their wing feathers and soar.

They steer with tail feathers.

All birds have feathers. But not all birds can fly.

An ostrich is too heavy to fly. But it can run very fast.

Penguins flap their wings underwater to swim. Their feathers keep them warm and dry.

Birds take care of their feathers. After flying, this tern preens its feathers. It uses its beak like a comb.

Birds Eat with Beaks

Birds need plenty of food to fly, run, or swim. You chew food with your teeth.

Birds don't have teeth. Birds use their beaks to eat. A hawk tears rabbit meat with its hook-shaped beak.

What will a heron catch?
It grabs fish with its long beak.

Woodpeckers tap holes in trees.

They pry insects from under a tree's bark.

Woodpeckers make a loud knock! They can drill deep holes in trees.

A flamingo sweeps its beak
from side to side in the water.

The flamingo
traps tiny plants
and animals in
its beak.

The flamingo's
beak is shaped
just right for
scooping.

Cardinals crack seeds with their thick beaks.

An oriole sits in her nest.

Birds Lay Eggs

When winter ends, many birds find safe places to lay eggs. Some build nests high in the trees. A mother oriole weaves her nest. She puts soft feathers inside. The father oriole sings in a nearby tree. He chases other birds away.

Puffins dig deep nests on high cliffs. The eggs will be safe there.

Terns build nests together in big groups called colonies. All the birds in a colony watch for danger.

These terns make their nest along the shore.

Baby birds grow inside eggs.
A mother bird warms them.
Chicks hatch from the eggs.

A baby robin hatches from its egg. It grew inside its egg for about thirteen days before hatching.

24

Barn swallow chicks chip open their eggs and climb out. The chicks cannot fly. Their parents bring them food.

Barn swallows tuck their nests in barns and outside buildings.

Loon chicks are born with down feathers. At two days old, they can swim and dive.

These loon chicks would rather ride on their mother's back.

Young robins grow flight feathers. They flap their wings.

They are ready to fly!

Find My Feet

Match the picture of the feet on page 28 with the bird on page 29.

a. Swimming feet

b. Perching feet

c. Hunting feet

d. Climbing feet

e. Running feet

A woodpecker uses its feet to climb up trees.

An emu's large feet have only three toes. They are strong for running fast.

An osprey swoops down to the water and grabs fish with its feet.

A parrot's feet hold onto tree branches.

A goose uses its feet to paddle across lakes.

Check your answers on page 31

Glossary

beak: a bird's bill

body feathers: feathers that cover and protect an adult bird's body. Body feathers give a bird its sleek shape and special colors.

chick: a baby bird

colony: a group of birds that builds nests near one another

down feathers: soft, fluffy feathers on a young bird. They are also the feathers that cover an adult bird's skin.

flight feathers: wing and tail feathers that birds use for flying

hatch: to break out of an egg

perching: holding and resting on a spot

preens: cleans feathers with a bird's beak

soar: to fly high in the sky

Further Reading

Aston, Dianna. *An Egg Is Quiet.* San Francisco: Chronicle Books, 2006.

Birds for Kids — Smithsonian National Zoological Park
http://nationalzoo.si.edu/Animals/Birds/ForKids

Jenkins, Martin. *The Emperor's Egg.* Cambridge, MA: Candlewick Press, 1999.

Jenkins, Priscilla Belz. *Falcons Nest on Skyscrapers.* New York: HarperCollins, 1996.

North American Birds
http://www.mrnussbaum.com/birdsindex.htm

Posada, Mia. *Guess What Is Growing Inside This Egg.* Minneapolis: Millbrook Press, 2007.

Underwood, Deborah. *Colorful Peacocks.* Minneapolis: Lerner Publications Company, 2007.

Answer key for pages 28–29:
a) a goose's feet,
b) a parrot's feet,
c) an osprey's feet,
d) a woodpecker's feet,
e) an emu's feet

Index

Photo Acknowledgments

The images in this book are used with the permission of: © Photodisc/Getty Images, pp. 1, 2, 5, 15; © Yetish Yetish/Alamy, p. 4; © chas53-Fotolia.com, p. 6; © Maslowski Productions, pp. 7, 8, 19, 24, 25, 28 (center and second from bottom), 29 (top and third from top); © Jennifer Daley/iStockphoto.com, p. 9; © Royalty-Free/CORBIS, p. 10; © kristian sekulic -Fotolia.com, p. 11; © Doug Allan/The Image Bank/Getty Images, p. 12; © BIOS Eichaker/ Peter Arnold, Inc., p. 13; © Undy-Fotolia.com , p. 16; © James Urbach/SuperStock, p. 17; © Oneworld-images-Fotolia.com, p. 18; © S. Muller/Peter Arnold, Inc., p. 20; © John Cornell/ Visuals Unlimited, Inc., p. 21; © Phillip Marazzi/Alamy, p. 22; Tom Mangelsen/naturepl.com, p. 23; © H. Schweiger/Peter Arnold, Inc., p. 26; © Wayne Lynch/DRK PHOTO, p. 27; © Nathalie PECQUEUR-Fotolia.com , p. 28 (top); © Tan Kian Khoon-Fotolia.com, p. 28 (second from top and bottom right); © Mark Newman/SuperStock, p. 28 (bottom); © seraphic06-Fotolia.com , p. 29 (second from top); © Pavie-Fotolia.com, p. 29 (bottom left); © age fotostock/SuperStock, pp. 30, 31.

Front cover: © Royalty-Free/Corbis (eagle and hummingbird); © Brand X Pictures (penguins).